RECORDING UNHINGED COLORING BOOK
FOR THOSE WHO COLOR OUTSIDE THE LINES

ILLUSTRATIONS BY SYLVIA MASSY
WITH CHRIS JOHNSON

Backbeat
Books

An Imprint of Hal Leonard LLC

T0351725

Copyright © 2016 by Sylvia Massy

All rights reserved. No part of this book may be reproduced in any form, without written permission, except by a newspaper or magazine reviewer who wishes to quote brief passages in connection with a review.

Published in 2016 by Backbeat Books
An Imprint of Hal Leonard LLC
7777 West Bluemound Road
Milwaukee, WI 53213

Trade Book Division Editorial Offices
33 Plymouth St., Montclair, NJ 07042

Printed in the United States of America

ISBN 978-1-4950-7671-8

www.backbeatbooks.com

COFFEE LOGIC

PRECISION

RICKENBACKER

DINGWALL

CHAPMAN

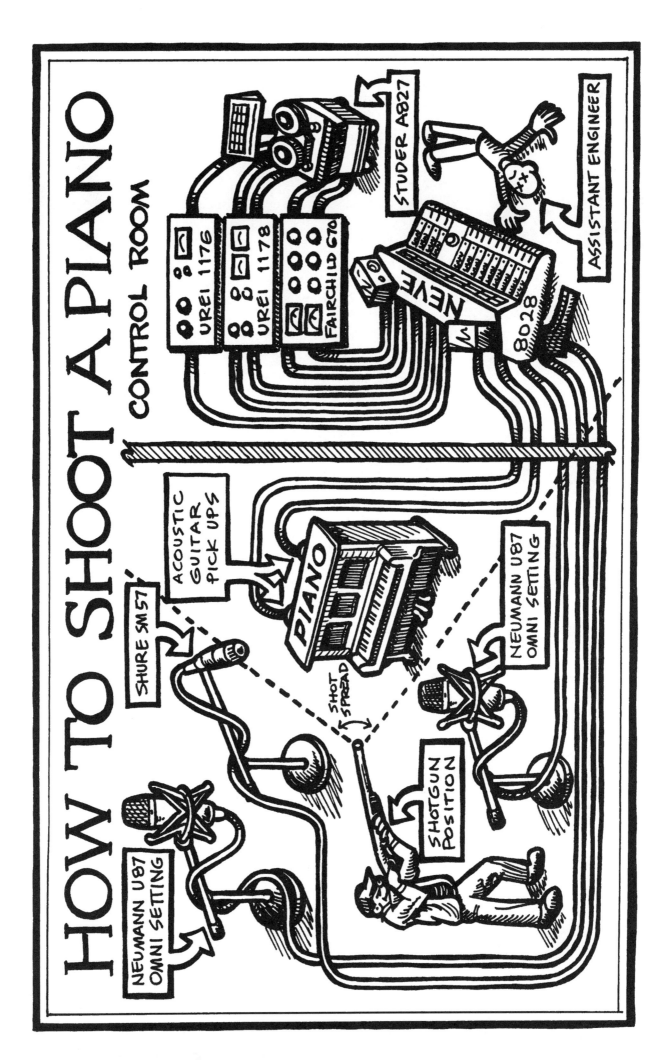

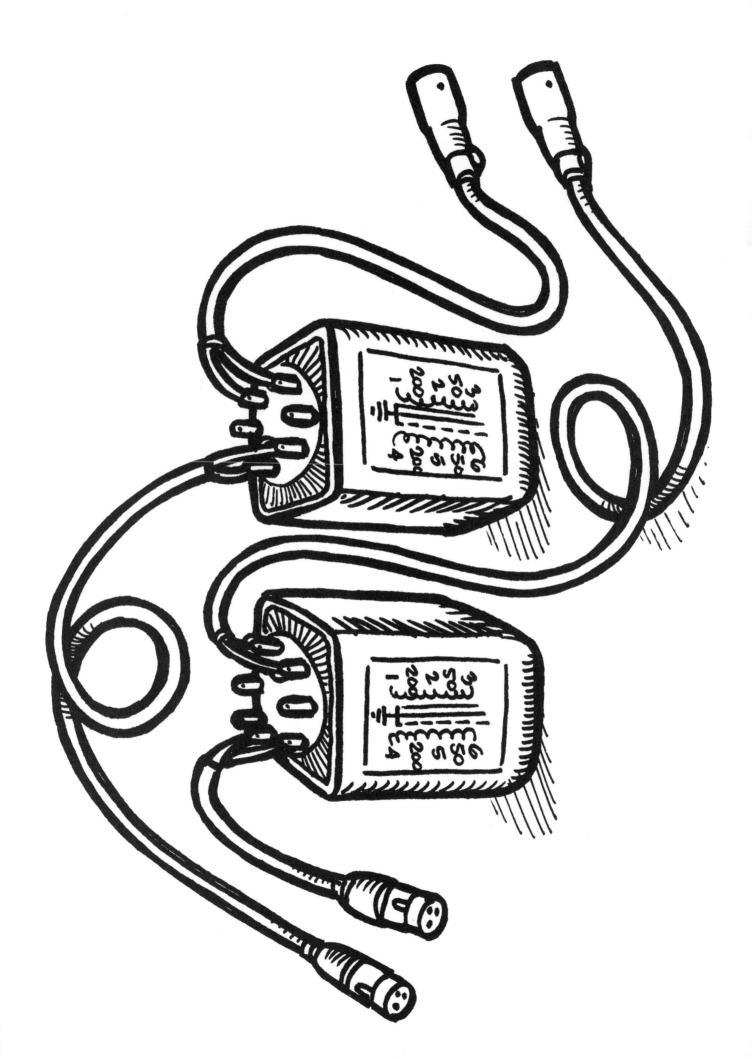

MEOW

DING - DONG

THUNDER

SIZZLE

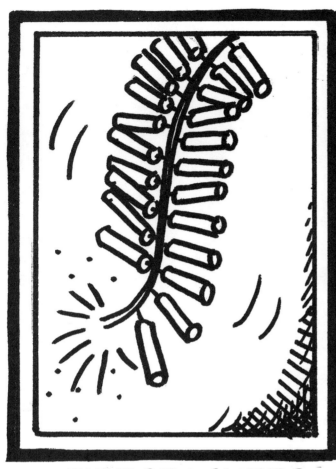

FIRECRACKERS

CAR DOORS

CHEESE GRATERS

BUTT BONGOS

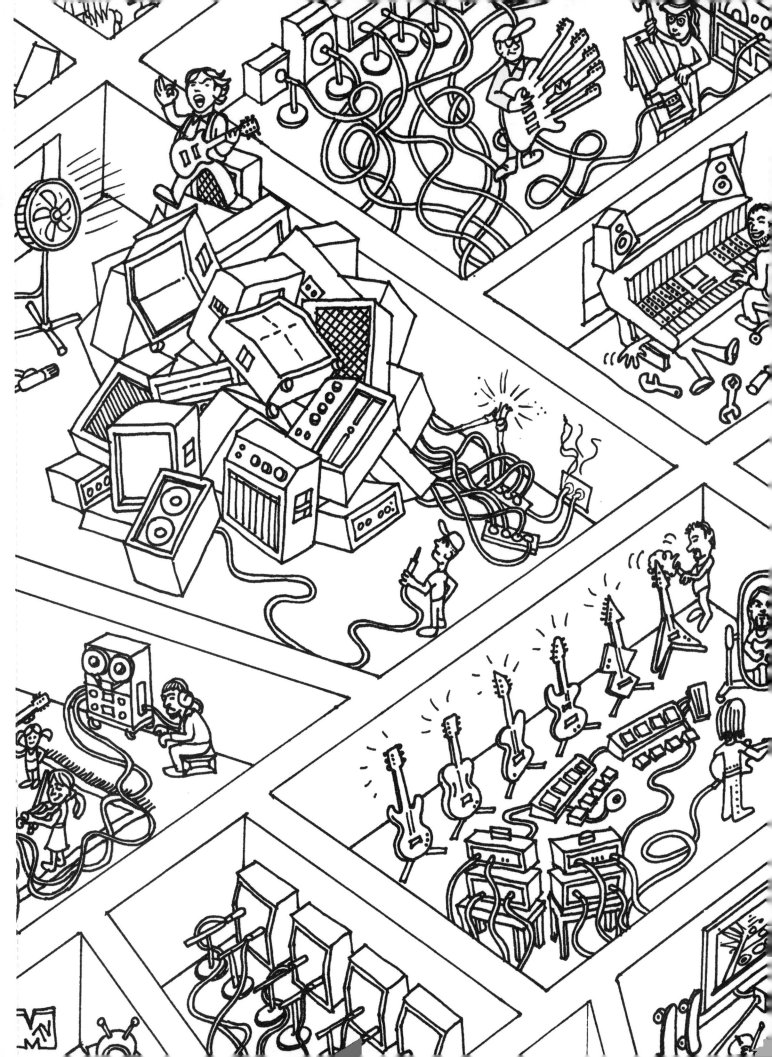

BOOM

POP

FOGHORN

BUBBLES

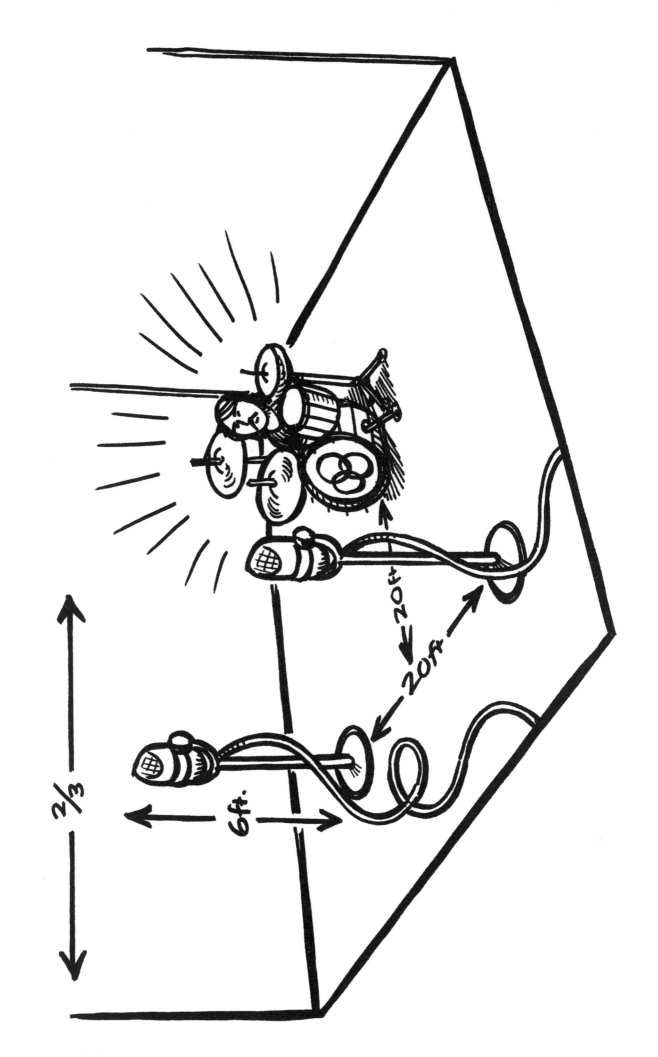

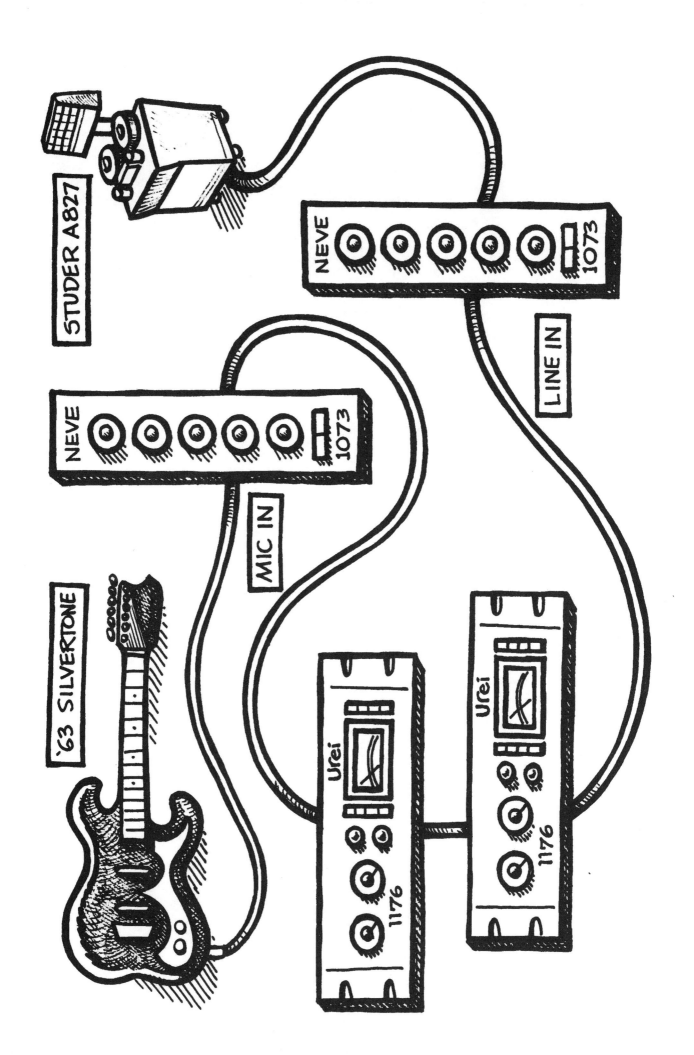

PRECISION

RICKENBACKER

DINGWALL

CHAPMAN

JUST THE
RIGHT AMOUNT OF TOO MUCH™

SING
UPSIDE DOWN

TURN OFF
THE LIGHTS

SING IN A
DINOSAUR SUIT

ALIEN
ABDUCTION

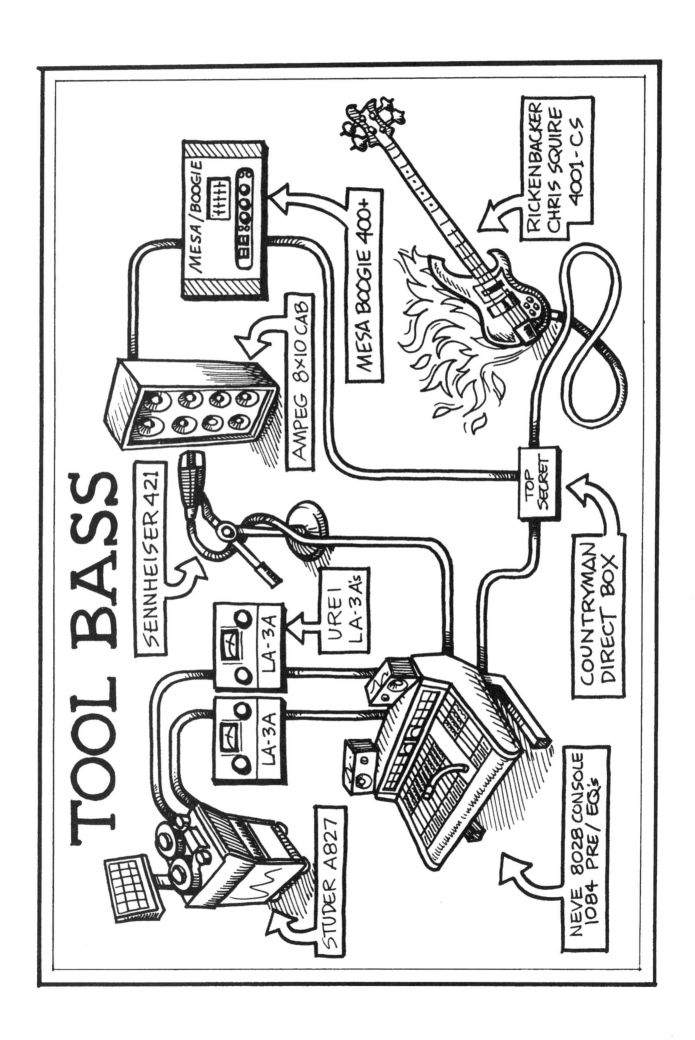

DINOSAUR BONES

WINE GLASSES

STEEL DRUMS

POWER TOOLS

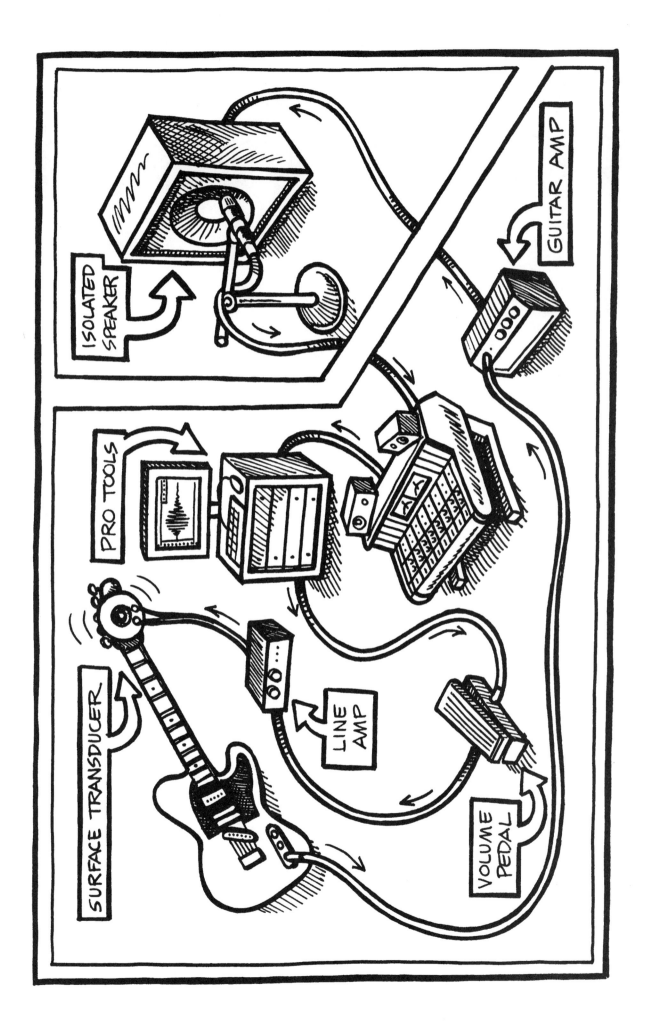

FLUSH

GHOSTS

TYPEWRITER

BUZZ

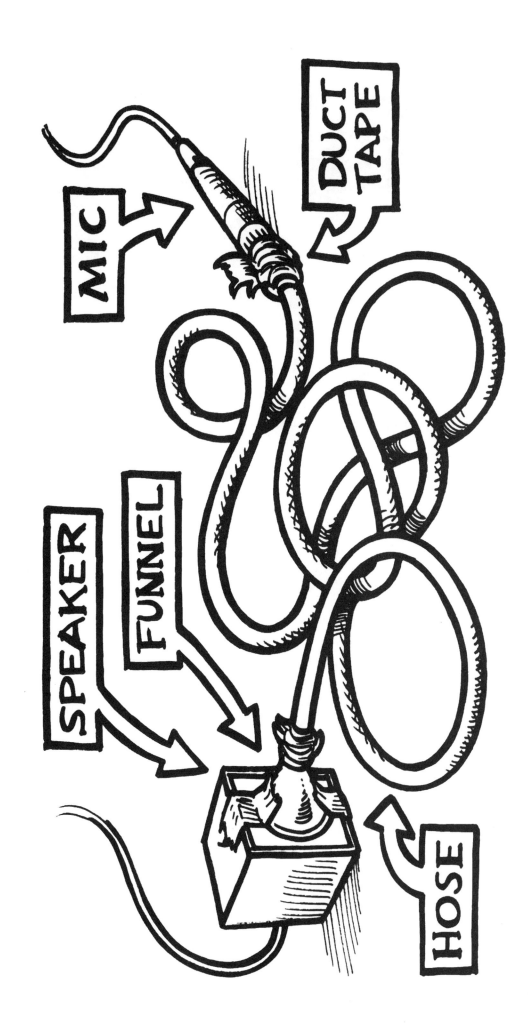

KNIFE
JUGGLING

TAPE SINGER
TO THE WALL

TURN ON
THE CAMERAS

BRING IN
A LADDER

A. ☒

B. ☒

C. ☑

HOW TIGHT IS YOUR
SPHINCTER?

PEDULLA

HOFNER

WARWICK

STEINBERGER

STUDIO BREW
by SYLVIA MASSY and CHRIS JOHNSON
GERMAN VALVE CONDENSER MICROPHONE
IS LIKE
FRENCH TRIPLE CREAM BRIE DE MEAUX
CREAMY, SMOOTH DELIGHTFUL CLASSIC
AMERICAN RIBBON VELOCITY MICROPHONE
EQUALS
DANISH BLUE ROQUEFORT PENICILLIUM AGED CHEESE
TANGY, BOLD - WITH A SOFT BITE
ENHANCED FREQUENCY RESPONSE DYNAMIC MICROPHONE
COMPARES TO
VERMONT PRIVATE STOCK CHEDDAR CHEESE
STURDY, SOLID = GOES WITH EVERYTHING
COMPACT USB MICROPHONE WITH DEMO TRIALWARE
SAME AS
PROCESSED CHEESE FOOD PRODUCT
Easy Whiz
I THINK I LIKE THEM ALL!
SOMETIMES EASY IS JUST TOO CHEESY
WWW.SYLVIAMASSY.COM

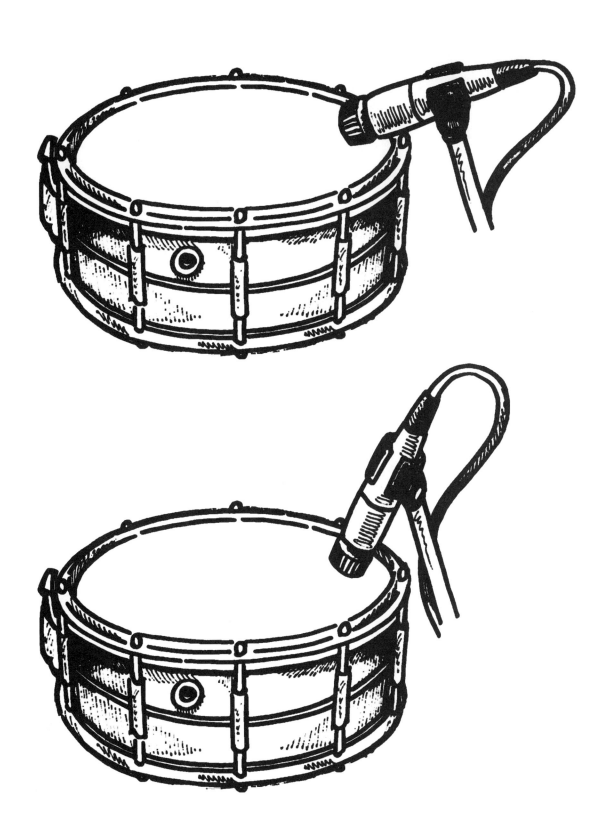

SILVERWARE

TOMMY GUNS

GNOME TASERS

FARTS

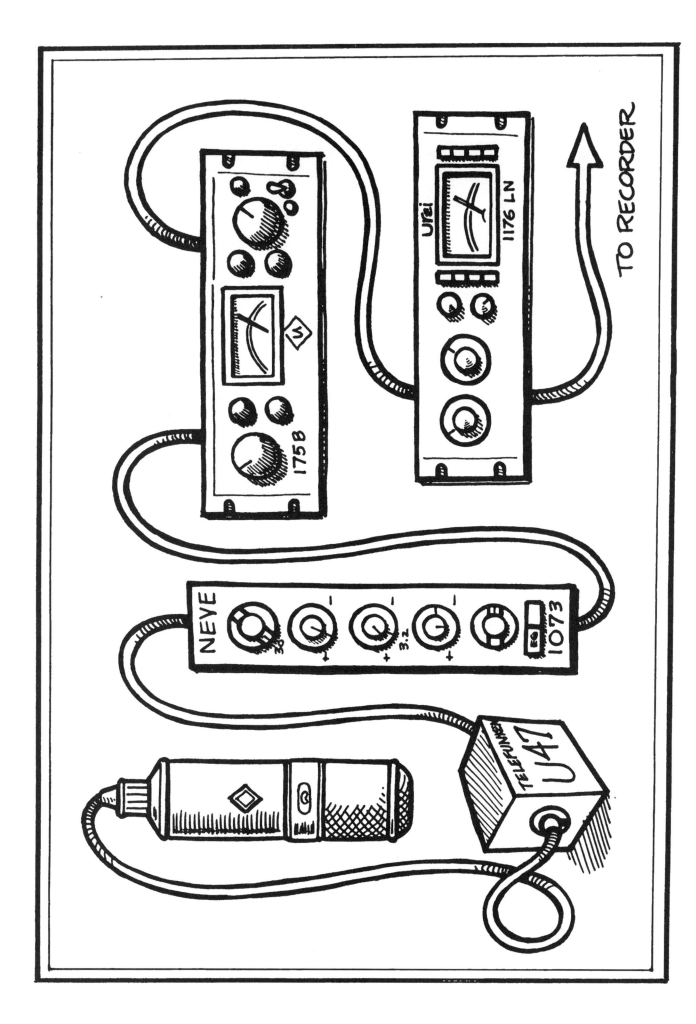

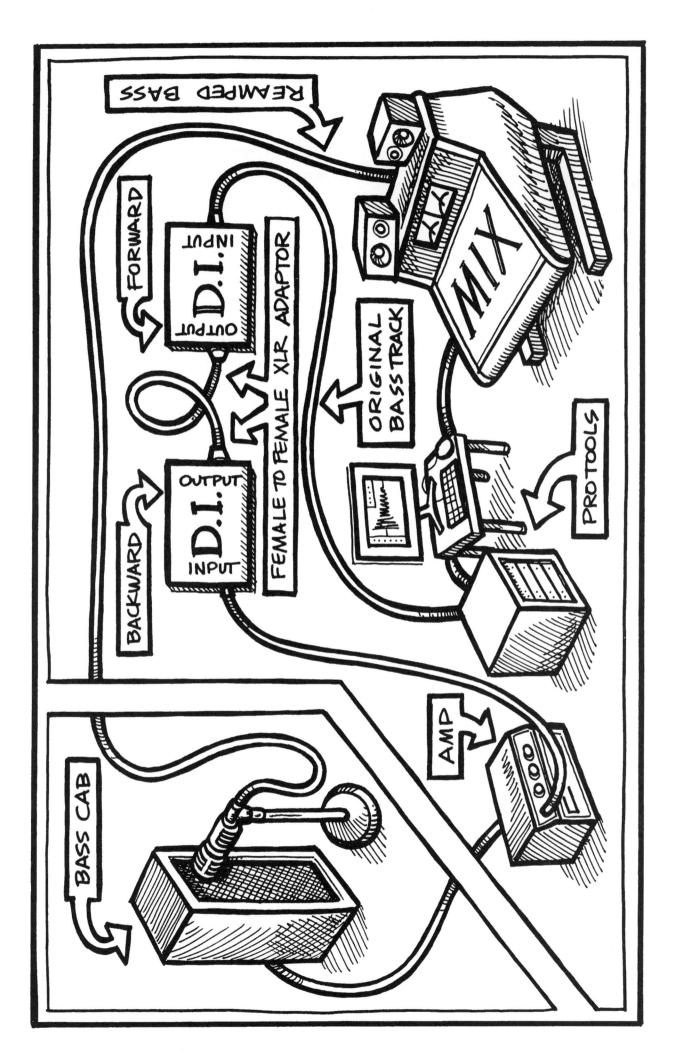

TICK - TOCK

HOOT

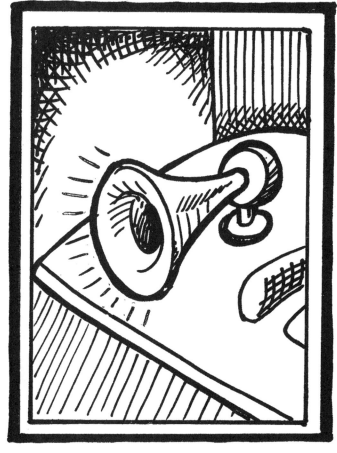

HONK

MOO

EVOLUTION OF BASS

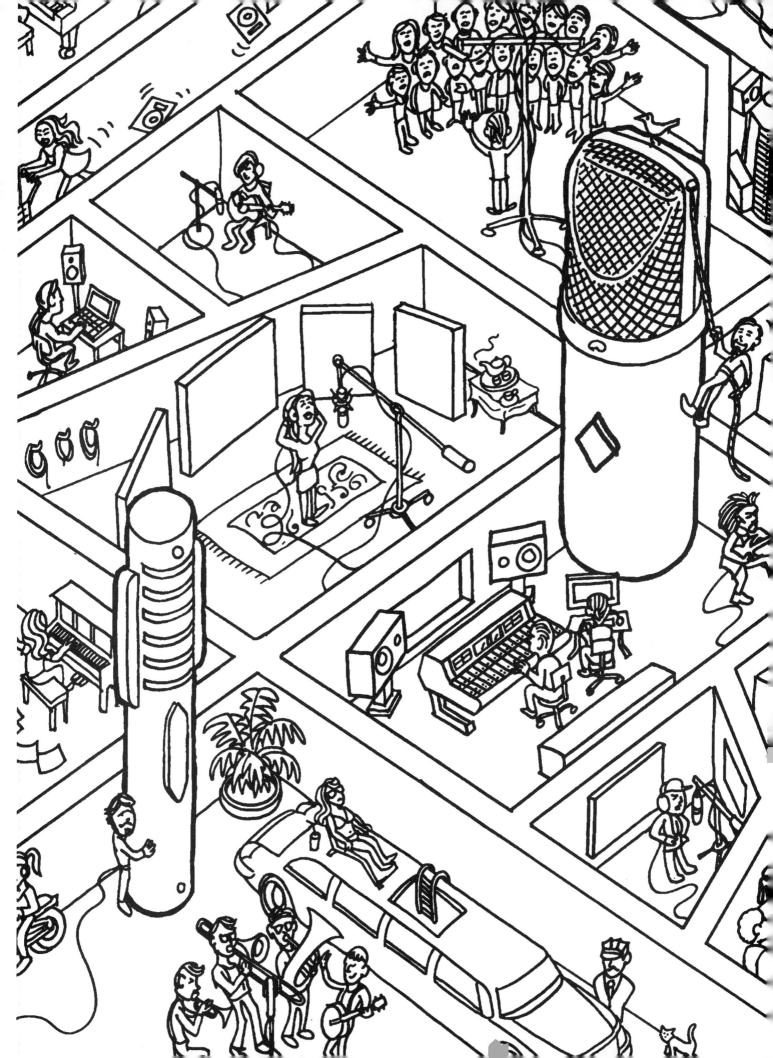

SHOCK
THERAPY

SING
NAKED

EXCESSIVE
EXCESS

SUBMERGE
VOCALIST

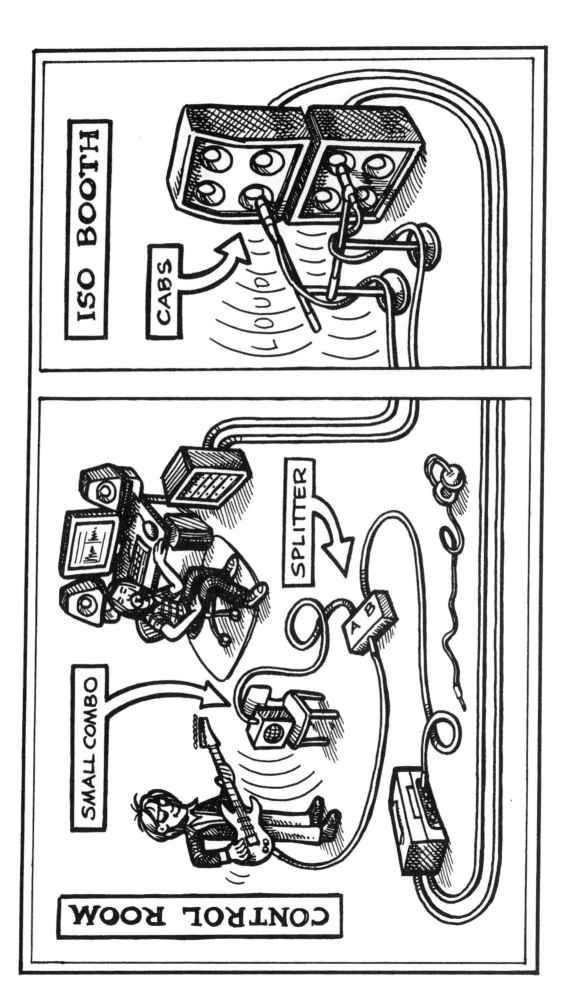

PRISON BARS

BICYCLE WHEELS

STEAM IRONS

TAP SHOES

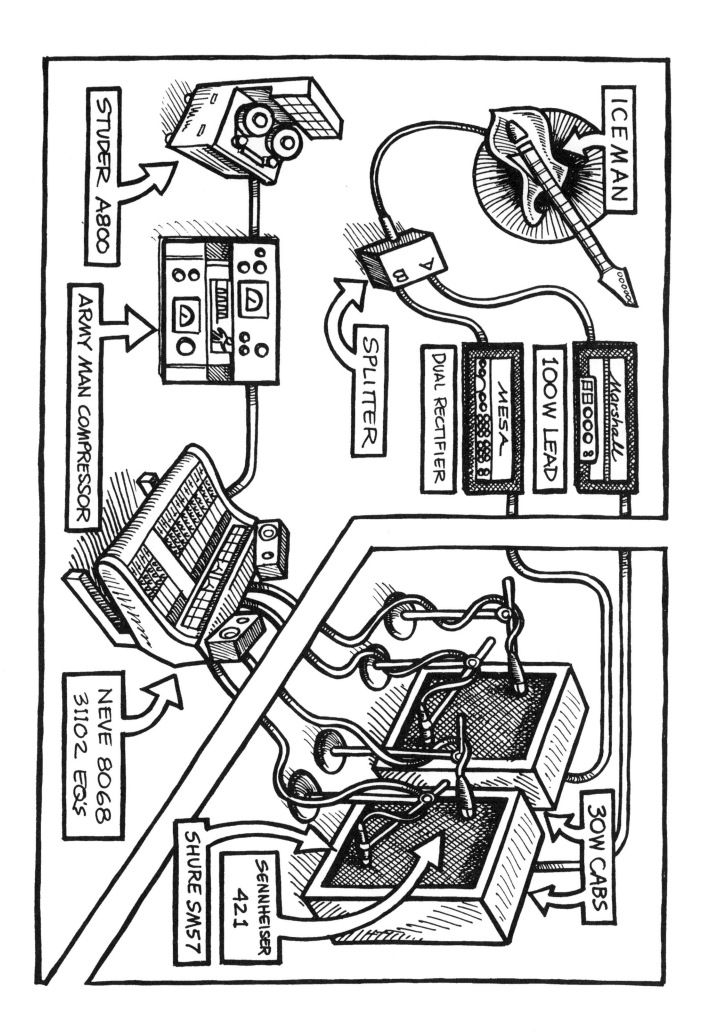

JAZZ

MODULUS

LONGHORN

MARCELINE

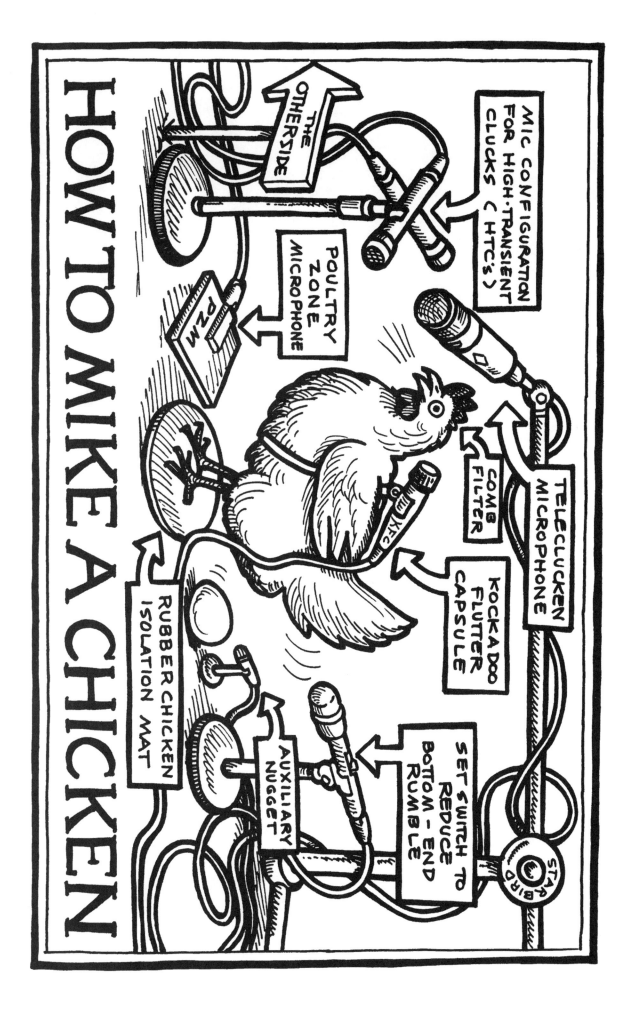